The Fishing Contest

The people in the big boat went out to sea.
Chug-chug-chug-chug

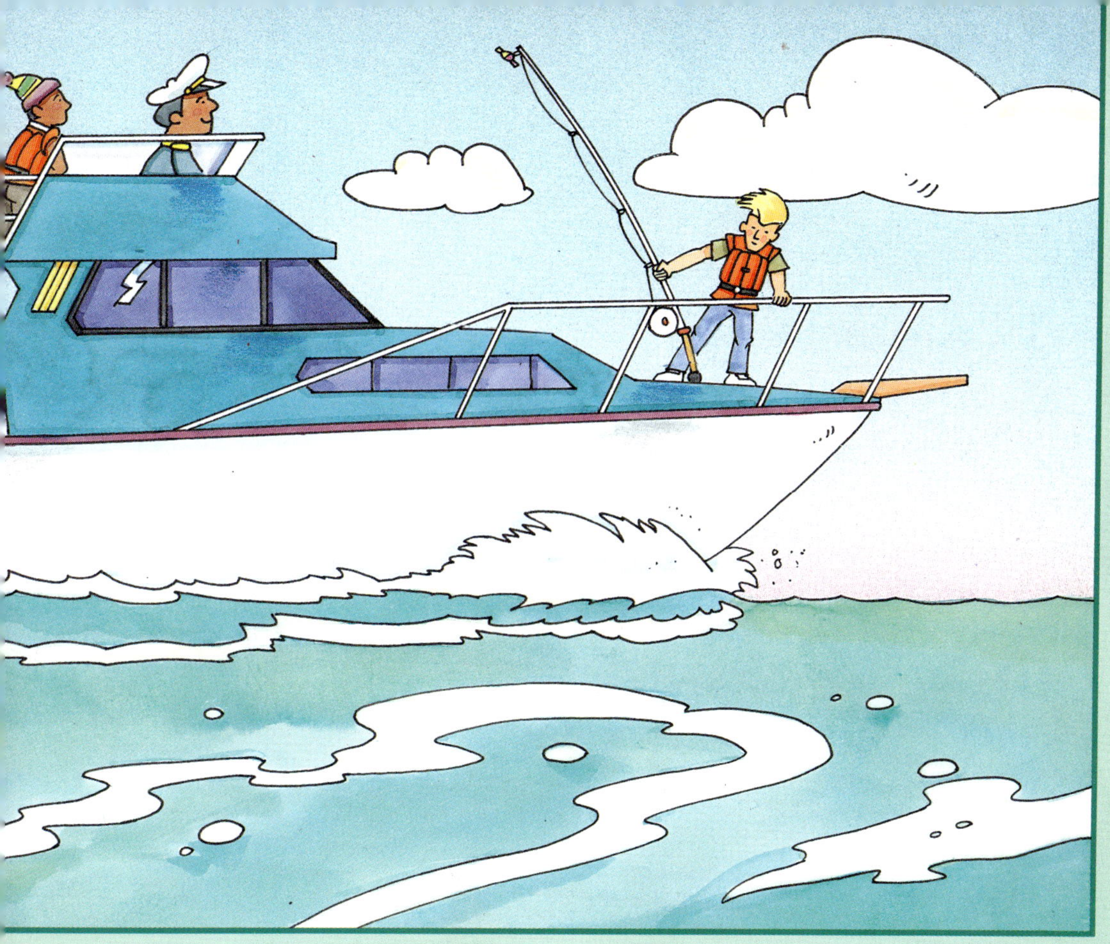

The people in the speedboat went out to sea.
Brmm-brmm-brmm-brmm

5

The people in the sailboat went out to sea.
Swish-swish-swish-swish

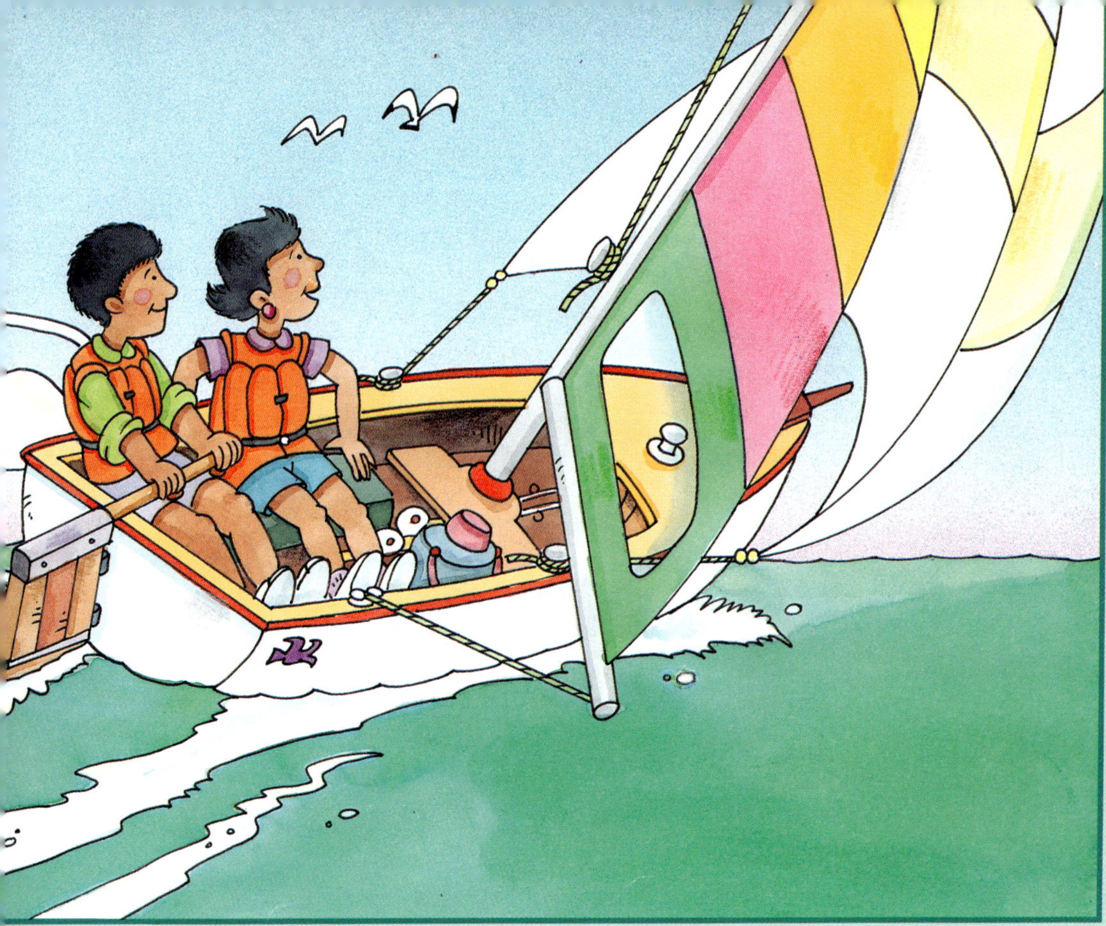

We went out to sea
in Grandad's little boat.
Putt-putt-putt-putt

We fished and fished all day.

The big boat came back.
Chug-chug-chug-chug

The speedboat came back.
Brmm-brmm-brmm-brmm

The sailboat came back.
Swish-swish-swish-swish

And we came back.
Putt-putt-putt-putt

In our boat was an enormous fish.

We won first prize.

We had fish for dinner.